CREEPY, KOOKY SCIENCE

Enemy Asteroids

Angie Timmons

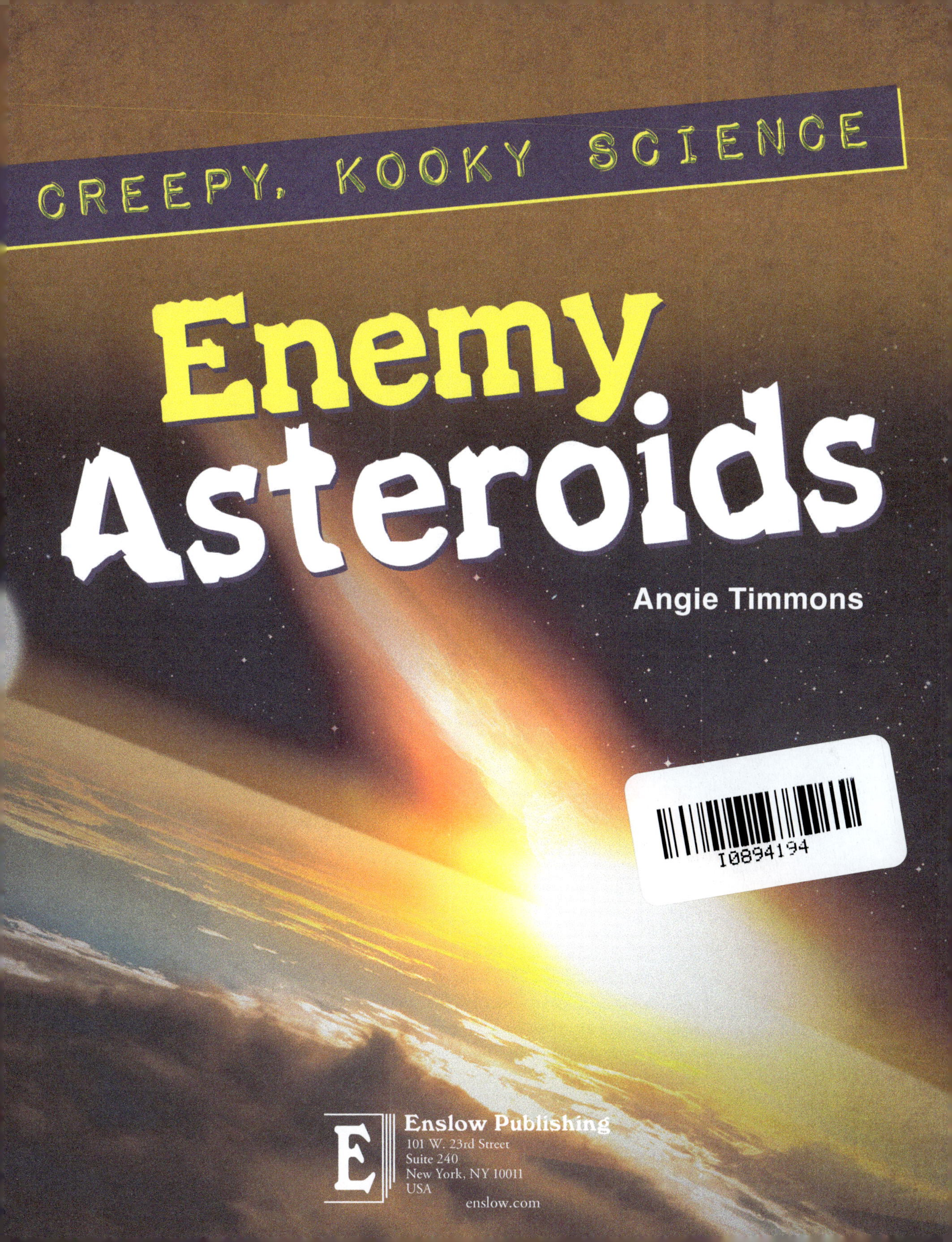

Enslow Publishing
101 W. 23rd Street
Suite 240
New York, NY 10011
USA
enslow.com

Published in 2019 by Enslow Publishing, LLC.
101 W. 23rd Street, Suite 240, New York, NY 10011

Library of Congress Cataloging-in-Publication Data

Names: Timmons, Angie, author.
Title: Enemy asteroids / Angie Timmons.
Description: New York : Enslow Publishing, [2019] | Series: Creepy, kooky science | Audience: Grades 5 to 8. | Includes bibliographical references and index.
Identifiers: LCCN 2018013874| ISBN 9781978503748 (library bound) | ISBN 9781978505490 (pbk.)
Subjects: LCSH: Asteroids—Collisions with Earth—Juvenile literature. | Asteroids—Juvenile literature.
Classification: LCC QB377 .T56 2018 | DDC 523.44—dc23
LC record available at https://lccn.loc.gov/2018013874

Printed in the United States of America

To Our Readers: We have done our best to make sure all websites in this book were active and appropriate when we went to press. However, the author and the publisher have no control over and assume no liability for the material available on those websites or on any websites they may link to. Any comments or suggestions can be sent by email to customerservice@enslow.com.

Portions of this book originally appeared in *Doomsday Rocks from Space* by Margaret Poynter.

Photo Credits: Cover, p. 1 muratart/Shutterstock.com; pp. 5, 21 NASA/Getty Images; p. 6 AF archive/Alamy Stock Photo; p. 8 Orla/Shutterstock.com; p. 9 tink-ivinki/Shutterstock.com; p. 10 Marcio Jose Bastos Silva/Shutterstock.com; p. 15 Joe Tucciarone/Science Source; p. 17 Nikolas_jkd/Shutterstock.com; pp. 18, 34 Detlev Van Ravenswaay/Science Photo Library/Getty Images; p. 24 John Thomas/Science Photo Library/Getty Images; p. 26 Anadolu Agency/Getty Images; p. 28 Cook Chris/ Science Source/Getty Images; pp. 37, 38 Corbis Historical/Getty Images.

Contents

Introduction

In the fall of 2003, enormous outbursts of energy from the sun triggered serious geomagnetic storms that caused mechanical and electrical issues on Earth. Because of high radiation storm levels, global organizations dedicated to the study of space took notice: "These events reminded scientists and policy makers alike how significantly the space environment can affect human society and its various space- and ground-based technologies."[1]

More than any other time in our history as a species, humans rely on technology for everything from microwaving food to using GPS to guide us while we travel to connecting through complex wireless networks. Any disruptions to those technologies could have serious consequences on every aspect of our lives, from inside our homes to the systems that keep order in the world's largest cities. The sun's hyperactivity back in 2003 only scratches the surface of the threats that come from space; while sun-related phenomena continue to pose threats to our ozone layers, we have historical evidence that other objects in space could be utterly devastating.

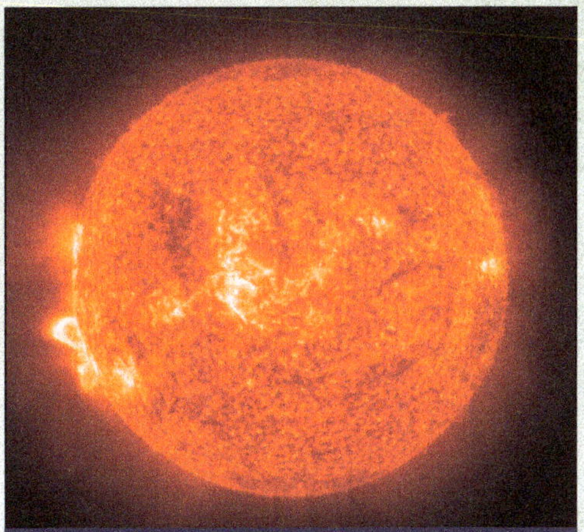

Fiery loops of hot gas (*lower left*) show the location of a 2003 solar flare that caused confusion in Earth's systems.

British scientist Richard Owen (1804–1892) realized in 1841 that the large bones and teeth being unearthed around the globe belonged not to some long-gone species of giant humans but rather to an ancient animal he called Dinosauria (which means "terrible lizards").[2] Since then, everyone from schoolchildren to top scientific experts have wondered what happened to these long-lost creatures.

The likely answer to the disappearance of the dinosaurs is a troubling one: an object from space interfered with Earth's atmosphere and climate so much that it caused their mass extinction. Even more troubling is the knowledge that something similar to whatever space hurtled at Earth during the time of the dinosaurs could pay Earth a visit in the future—endangering all species, including humans, and plant life and our delicate ecosystems. This "Armageddon," which is a biblical reference to the end of days, has for generations been at the forefront of everything from scientific experiments to Hollywood's imagination. Two of the most

In the 1998 movie *Deep Impact*, an astronomer realizes a comet is on a collision course with Earth and tries to save civilization from extinction.

popular movies of the 1990s, *Armageddon* and *Deep Impact,* told stories of human interventions to stop Earth's collision with massive space objects that could cause annihilation.

While audiences have certainly been captivated by the space drama depicted in such movies, the drama is, in fact, real: through astronomy, we know space is home to many threats, small and large. We've become familiar with some space objects, such as Halley's comet, which gets close enough to Earth for us to see it every seventy-six or so years. If Earth crossed paths with Halley, we could be exposed to deadly toxic gases. But what about other threats, such as asteroids, which are millions of minor planets that stay relatively close to the sun? An asteroid that's just 6 miles (10 kilometers) wide would "punch through the atmosphere like it's hardly even there," destroying most of Earth's surface and causing a debris cloud that would block the sun. Almost everything on Earth would die.[3]

Knowing what we know, what do we do now about these enemies from space?

CHAPTER 1

When Dinosaurs Roamed

For almost 180 million years, a group of reptiles ruled Earth. These reptiles were often large, and they lived pretty much everywhere: in mountainous areas, in the plains, in deserts, in forests, and in swamps and other bodies of water, on nearly every continent—places we now know as North America and Europe.

We now know this group of reptiles as the dinosaurs, which appeared roughly 245 million years ago.[1] These creatures shared their world with other types of reptiles and with insects, frogs, turtles, snails, and small mammals.

Dinosaurs came in many different shapes and sizes. Some walked on all fours. Some were so heavy that they lived in swamps where the water could support their bodies. Still others stood on their hind legs, balanced by their tails.

Some dinosaurs were much bigger than humans. This artwork shows a Tyrannosaurus rex (*left*), an Albertaceratops (*right*), and two Pterodactyls soaring above them.

There were dinosaurs that were only 2 feet (0.6 meters) long. One of the largest may have been 125 feet (38 m) long. Some were as tall as a six-story building. It is believed that the heaviest dinosaur weighed more than 50 tons (100,000 pounds or 45,359 kilograms).[2]

Some dinosaurs ate meat and others survived on diets of leaves and grass.

It used to be thought that all dinosaurs were cold-blooded creatures; they needed the sun to warm them up like reptiles and amphibians today. Now it is thought that at least some of the dinosaurs were warm-blooded.[3] Like human beings, they produced their own heat when their muscles burned the food they ate.

Dinosaurs and the Supercontinent

The world of the dinosaurs was very different from the world of today. There were reptiles everywhere—on the land, in lakes, in the sea, and in the air. There were few hot or cold areas. In most places, the climate was warm and balmy.

At the beginning of the dinosaurs' reign, all of Earth's land was lumped together in one mass, dotted with small inland seas. This single landmass was called Pangaea by German scientist Alfred Wegener (1880–1930).[4] There were no great oceans to interrupt the animals' movements and no towering mountain ranges to block their paths.

Pangaea was a supercontinent that existed during the late Paleozoic and early Mesozoic eras.

Earth's surface is made up of interlocking plates, which are sections of land. These plates are always on the move. Because of this movement, Pangaea began to break up about two hundred million years ago. Huge chunks of land drifted away. Those pieces became the seven continents. Great mountain ranges rose when continents collided. The inland seas drained into the ocean. In some places, the mild climate became cold. In others, it became much warmer. The average temperature rose by as much as twenty degrees.

Over millions of years, some places got drier or wetter, colder or hotter. Dinosaurs and other animals moved to different places. In the hot areas, the dinosaurs could not cool off. They had no sweat glands to release their body heat. As time passed, some dinosaurs died from the heat and lack of water.

Most dinosaurs, however, evolved with their new environments. Their senses were keen, they were alert and aggressive, and they

Fossils can tell us much about life before humans, including where and how different species of dinosaurs lived.

were very adaptable. The world was changing, but the dinosaurs still ruled that world.

A Decade of Darkness

Then, about sixty-six million years ago, catastrophe struck. In one area, there was a huge explosion—an unknown object had smashed into Earth. Dinosaurs grazing nearby were killed instantly. The impact of the explosion was probably felt hundreds of miles away. The initial heat blast may have killed many dinosaurs. Then, tons of dust, ash, and soot filled the atmosphere. For months, the heat and light of the sun could not penetrate this dust cloud. The skies were dark, and Earth grew colder and colder. There were snowstorms.

Blundering about in the darkness, the remaining herbivores stripped the trees of every last leaf. Some of the hardier ones survived for a time by

The Long Night, Nuclear Warfare, and Human-made Destruction

Using a computer model, scientists are studying the effects of the 6-mile-wide (10 km wide) object that struck Earth and started the decade of darkness to better understand how the atmosphere would be impacted by nuclear warfare and the subsequent "nuclear winter."[5]

Other scientists believe human-made changes to the environment—especially the ever-increasing destruction of natural habitats that causes species to go extinct—through overpopulation and exploitation of natural resources will bring on the next mass extinction of life on Earth.[6]

We don't just need an answer for the threats from space—we need to solve the problems we're causing right here on Earth, right now.

digging through the snow for grass and moss. They ate twigs and chewed the bark off dead trees. Eventually, even that food supply was gone.

The surviving carnivores continued to feast on their starving plant-eating cousins and other mammals. When there was no more prey, the ravenous creatures turned on each other.

As time passed, the dust cloud began to disappear. Within ten years, it was gone. This caused sweltering temperatures. After this, the dinosaurs became extinct, as had at least two thirds of the other plant and animal species living on Earth. The course of evolution had been changed forever.

What caused the sudden, drastic events that led to the destruction of the dinosaurs? Could such a disaster ever occur again? To find the answers to those questions, scientists have looked for clues on Earth and in outer space.

CHAPTER 2

The Tunguska Event

Spanning 5,772 miles (9,289 km), the Trans-Siberian Railway connects Russia's capital city, Moscow, to the Russian Far East, which is encompassed by a huge region called Siberia.[1] This region's vast wildernesses and harsh winters leave much of it sparsely populated. It was in one such sparsely populated area that the world's longest rail line encountered an explosive event in which Earth faced off with space.

On the morning of June 30, 1908, the Trans-Siberian Express was making its regular run across the vast plains of northern Russia. Its conductor was startled to hear a series of loud bangs, and he wondered if there had been an accident.[2] After stopping the train, he rushed back to the passenger car. There, a group of wide-eyed men and women said that they had heard what sounded like explosions and had seen a bright blue ball of flame streaking across the sky. It had left a trail of smoke behind it.

Residents of the sparsely populated area had also seen and heard the explosion. Some of them lived near the 830 square miles (2,150 sq km) of forest that had been uprooted by the shock waves. Thirty miles (48 km) away, others saw the bodies of the reindeer that had been killed by the blast. The tents of nomads camping several miles away were scattered. The clothes of a man who had been standing 60 miles (97 km) away caught on fire.

At the time of the event, Russia was a hotbed of civil strife. Scientists could not safely travel to Siberia until the 1920s. Once they finally got to travel to Siberia, they found the remains of the massive fallen forest. They saw small remnants of an object scattered over a wide area, as well as several small holes caused by the remnants upon landing on Earth's surface.

Most experts believe an asteroid, a small, planet-like space object, entered the atmosphere, where a combination of heat and pressure fragmented the asteroid and destroyed it—producing the fireball witnessed that early morning in 1908 over Siberia.

Referred to as the Tunguska event because of its proximity to the Stony Tunguska River, the phenomenon took place a little more than 5 miles (8 km) up in the atmosphere, producing a fireball, a cloud of dust, and tiny fragments. The explosion had the force of an estimated 12 million tons of TNT, a powerful explosive.

In 1908, an object from space entered Earth's atmosphere, creating a fireball that disrupted operations in Siberia, Russia, with a huge explosion.

Its impact was equivalent to about 185 Hiroshima bombs—the atomic bomb that leveled Hiroshima in 1945 to end World War II.[3]

Did Something from the Sky Kill the Dinosaurs?

Items from space have been falling on Earth for billions of years and will continue falling as long as Earth exists.

Each day, three or four 20-pound (9-kg) meteorites—pieces of rocky or metallic debris—strike Earth's surface. (Naturally occurring objects that enter Earth's orbit, such as meteorites, are sometimes called "debris" because they're pieces or fragments of a larger object, such as a meteor. This type of debris should not be confused with space debris, with is created by human-made objects.) Once every hundred years, a 4,000-ton meteorite falls from the sky, and once every one hundred thousand years, a meteorite weighing 50,000 tons or more plows into our small planet.

Earth's surface is scarred by at least 100 craters that resulted from collisions with large space objects. Only fifty thousand years ago, a 150-foot-wide (46 m wide) nickel-iron meteorite smashed into what is now northern Arizona. At impact, it was traveling about 25,000 miles (40,000 km) per hour. The force of the collision sent 300 million tons of rock flying high into the air. It left a vast crater 660 feet deep (201 m) and about 4,000 feet (1,200 m) wide. That crater could swallow a sixty-story building or hold eleven football fields.

Such a large object causes a lot of damage to the environment. Could a

What's Space Debris?

In January 2007, the Chinese military destroyed its Fengyun-1C weather satellite, creating more than three thousand fragments suspended in Earth's orbit. Six years later, Russian scientists had to abandon a mission using a laser-ranging satellite, BLITS, when the satellite experienced a sudden orbit and spin change. Scientists believe a fragment from the Fengyun satellite collided with BLITS and completely disrupted its path.

The Fengyun fragments are part of hundreds of thousands of human-made, defunct materials called space debris that orbit Earth for years before re-entering the atmosphere. Because objects in Earth's orbit travel at high speeds, even a tiny piece of debris poses a threat to spacecrafts.[4]

The meteor crater left in Arizona is fifty thousand years old and 150 feet (46 m) wide.

meteorite have led to the extinction of the dinosaurs? For many years, scientists tried to answer that question. In the late 1970s, Walter Alvarez (1940–), an American geologist, was in Italy. He was studying a thin layer of clay that lay between two layers of rock. This same layer of clay exists in various parts of the world. The rock above the clay had been formed later than the rock below it. The clay marked the boundary between two geologic eras. A geologic era is a period of time in history. Each era is marked by distinctive types of rock and rock formations.

As Alvarez poked and pried into the bottom layer of rock, he found dinosaur fossils embedded in it. He then examined the upper layer of rock. In that layer, there were no such fossils. That layer of clay must have been formed at the same time that the dinosaurs vanished.

The meteorite impact at Chicxulub on the Yucatán Peninsula in Mexico may have caused the extinction of the dinosaurs and 70 percent of all of Earth's species sixty-six million years ago.

Later, other scientists studied samples of the same clay. One of them was Walter's father, Luis, a physicist. The team made an important and exciting discovery: there were traces of iridium in the clay. Iridium is a metal that is seldom found naturally on Earth's surface. It is, however, often found in meteorites.

The Rock That Doomed the Dinosaurs?

Other geologic studies found iridium in the same layer of clay in other parts of the world. There were also bits of glassy rock called tektites, which are formed when asteroid debris mixes with superhot gases. These and other discoveries led to a startling conclusion: sixty-six million years ago, a giant asteroid 6.2 miles (9.9 km) wide must have slammed into Earth. When the huge, fast-moving object plowed into the ground, there was a rapid release of energy.

That energy was converted into heat. Most of the asteroid vaporized; it changed into gas. The rocks close by the crash scene were also vaporized. The vapor expanded and exploded. The blast was ten thousand times more powerful than the combined explosions of all the nuclear weapons in the world today. It left a deep crater in the ground. The dust and debris from the crater were thrown high into the atmosphere.

Many experts believe they know the exact spot where the asteroid crashed to Earth.[5] This spot is in what is now Mexico's Yucatán Peninsula. There, a mile (1.6 km) underground, lies a circular crater 190 miles (306 km) wide. Scientific testing of rock samples taken from the rim of this mammoth hole shows that this rock had melted suddenly, as it would in an explosion, and then hardened.

Studies showed that this melted rock was formed sixty-six million years ago, when the layer of clay was formed. It was at this same time that the dinosaurs disappeared from Earth.

CHAPTER 3

Space Rocks Zooming By

Though the circumstances around why the dinosaurs disappeared are still not fully understood, the dinosaurs aren't the only species to have suddenly disappeared. Throughout history, other species have vanished suddenly, and scientists know some of those vanishings were linked to space objects that collided with Earth.

It is not surprising that these collisions occur because Earth is like a spaceship. Traveling 65,000 miles (105,000 km) per hour, it makes continuous voyages around the sun. Earth is not alone in its travels: whizzing past Earth in the same or the opposite direction, there are specks of dust and grains of sand, pebbles, small rocks, and boulders as large as trucks or houses.

"Starlike" Planets: Asteroids

In space, there are also huge chunks of stone or metal; some are the size of mountains, others the size of small cities. The largest of these "flying mountains" is 600 miles (nearly 1,000 km) in diameter. These miniature planets have craters from past impacts with other large objects.

Through a telescope, these larger pieces of space rubble look like points of light. The ancient Greeks thought they were stars. Today, we call them asteroids, which is Greek for "starlike." Asteroids are leftovers from the creation of our solar system 4.5 billion years ago. Some are pieces that were chipped off another asteroid during a collision. Some asteroids are made of rock and others have cores of dense metal. Some have smaller asteroids orbiting around them.

NASA's Dawn spacecraft took this image of the asteroid called Vesta from about 3,200 miles (5,150 km) above its surface in July 2011.

The asteroid belt lies between Mars and Jupiter, where there is plenty of room. Their orbits may remain stable for millions of years. Sometimes, however, two asteroids collide. In this game of cosmic billiards, one of them gets knocked out of its orbit. Eventually, it is caught by the gravity of a larger body. It may keep traveling in a shortened orbit, or it may collide with the larger body. Most of the craters on the moons and planets of our solar system are the result of collisions with asteroids.

Earth's gravity pulls a few asteroids into our planet's neighborhood. Currently, there are more than a hundred known asteroids whose orbits cross Earth's orbit. An asteroid travels at 10 to 30 miles (16 to 48 km) a second. When a building-sized asteroid smacks into our atmosphere, friction heats it up to thousands of degrees. When it gets hot enough, it blows up with a blinding flash of light called a meteor.

From Earth, these meteors, or shooting stars, appear to be streaks of light across the night sky. The smaller meteors disappear from view in the blink of an eye. The larger ones look like bright fireballs. The remnants leave a blazing trail across the sky.

Mammoth fireballs can be created when asteroids explode. At such times, powerful shock waves ripple through Earth's atmosphere. One such event took place high above Indonesia in 1988. The force of the explosion was calculated to be equal to that of five thousand tons of high explosives. Seen from Earth, the meteor looked like a flash of light as bright as the sun.

Tiny Solar Systems: Comets

Astronomers classify comets according to how long they take to orbit the sun. Short-period comets, which come from the Kuiper belt beyond the orbit of Pluto, need less than two hundred years to complete one orbit. Long-period comets take two hundred years or longer. Long-period comets begin in a region even farther (maybe a thousand times farther) beyond Pluto's orbit called the Oort cloud.

At first, comets look like tumbling dirty snowballs. The core is less than 10 miles (16 km) across. At this stage, they are too far away to be seen from Earth.

Occasionally, a group of young comets is snared by the gravity from a passing star. The comets then travel in an orbit that plunges them from their birthplace toward the sun. During this journey, they pass by Jupiter or Saturn. The paths of some of the comets are changed by the gravity of these planets.

About once every century, a comet careens toward the inner solar system.

The Quick Rundown of Space Objects

Asteroids are large objects (more than 32 feet [10 m] wide) that orbit the sun and are made of rock or metal.

Comets are bodies of ice, rock, and dust that orbit the sun and can be several miles in diameter. Asteroids or comet debris are usually the source of meteoroids, small rocky or metal objects that orbit the sun. When Earth passes through a trail of comet debris, a group of meteors called a meteor shower is visible.

A meteor, or "shooting star," is a meteoroid that enters Earth's atmosphere and vaporizes.

A meteorite is a meteor that hits Earth without vaporizing in the atmosphere.[1]

The comet called Hyakutake, which passed within 9.3 million miles (15 million km) of Earth in 1996, was one of the brightest comets to appear in the sky during the twentieth century.

Somewhere between Jupiter and Mars, the sun's heat turns the comet's frozen gases into vapor. The vapor, combined with particles of ice, streams out behind the comet's core, forming a dust tail.

The core of the comet erupts with great puffs of gas and dust. Like the thrusters on a spacecraft, these puffs cause a very slow change in the comet's orbit. The comet may enter our inner solar system because of its original orbit or the gravitational pull of other planets.

Only a few such stragglers are ever seen from Earth. By that time, they are very old comets. The warmth of the sun is causing them to come apart. Eventually, all the ice melts. All that remains are the rock and dust that form the core. The comet then resembles an asteroid.

An entire comet can fill a space much larger than Earth. The cloud of gas and dust that surrounds the comet's core can be larger than the sun. Despite its size, a comet has very little mass. This lack of mass means that it does not exert much gravitational pull. It passes closely to moons and planets without disturbing them at all.

On the other hand, a comet can easily be pulled off course by a giant planet—Jupiter, Saturn, or Uranus. It then becomes locked into a shorter orbit and approaches the sun at regular intervals. With each approach, the sun's heat causes more of the comet's ice to melt. The more ice that melts, the shorter the comet's life span becomes.

About two hundred of these periodic comets visit Earth's cosmic neighborhood regularly. The most famous is Halley's comet, which reappears every seventy-six to seventy-nine years.

Another periodic comet is called Swift-Tuttle. It was seen in 1862, then again spotted in September 1992. On November 7, 1992, it passed within 110 million miles (177 million km) of Earth. Each August, Earth crosses Swift-Tuttle's orbit. Even though the comet itself is far away on its 130-year journey around the sun,

This photo of the Perseid meteor shower was taken in Turkey in 2015. As Earth passes through debris from the Swift-Tuttle comet, meteors appear as streaks of light from the constellation Perseus in the northeastern sky.

the particles it left behind remain in orbit. When Earth crosses the orbit, the particles burn up in the atmosphere. From the ground, the burning particles appear to be streaks of light. This event is called the Perseid meteor shower. It is one of the most spectacular annual meteor showers.

It has been predicted that Swift-Tuttle will return to Earth's area of space on August 14, 2126. On that date, it will come much closer to our planet than it did in 1992. One astronomer figured it may come within 14 million miles (23 million km) of Earth, moving at 130,000 miles (209,170 km) per hour.[2]

CHAPTER 4

Stopping a Doomsday Rock

The rock that doomed the dinosaurs was probably about the same size as the core of Swift-Tuttle: about 5 miles (8 km) across. What will happen if Swift-Tuttle changes its course even a little bit? What if the jets that propel it edge it toward Earth?

For a while, astronomers thought Earth might be in danger in 2126. Now they believe Swift-Tuttle will not be a real threat until 3044.[1] If it strikes Earth's surface, so much dust will be thrown into our atmosphere that all crops will die. Many of the world's animals will perish. Very few human beings will survive. The survivors may have to live as our cave-dwelling ancestors lived. They will have to pick berries and dig roots. With luck, they will find a pig or a cow to eat.

The comet Swift-Tuttle could have a devastating impact on Earth.

Swift-Tuttle could become Earth's doomsday rock; so could at least one hundred other asteroids whose orbits now cross that of our planet. On the average, an object two-thirds of a mile (one kilometer) wide will strike Earth once every one million years. An object 1.2 miles (2 km) wide will strike our planet once every few million years.

Our moon bears the scars of such collisions; so do the other planets and their moons. On Earth, however, it appears that those space objects did more than just leave scars. It may have been a visiting comet that furnished the molecules needed for life to develop.[2] Our oceans may have been produced in part by a watery invader from outer space.

What about the dinosaurs' doomsday rock? Before it struck, many primitive mammals fell prey to giant predators. The extinction of the dinosaurs cleared the way for the mammals to thrive and develop, eventually leading to the appearance of the first human beings.

If those humans had been forced to share their planet with giant meat-eating reptiles, they would not have survived. The dinosaurs would still be ruling Earth.

Warding Off the Ultimate Disaster

So far, a large comet or asteroid has not landed in a highly populated area, but what if the object that exploded over Siberia in 1908 had slammed into a large city? It could have destroyed hundreds of buildings and killed tens of thousands of people.

Experts agree that sometime in the future, such an object could cause either a local or a worldwide catastrophe.[3] If nothing is done, human beings might go the way of the dinosaurs. The difference is that prehistoric creatures could not save themselves.

Because of modern scientific knowledge, we are now aware of the danger. The challenge is to use that knowledge to prevent what could be Earth's final disaster. The first step is to identify all possible doomsday rocks. Scientists use many tools, such

Other Space Threats to Life on Earth

Scientists are keeping their eyes on threats such as high-energy solar flares, which can impact radio communication and electricity; local gamma ray bursts, which are powerful energy bursts that can cause radiation that destroys our ozone layer; supernovas, which are explosions that happen when a star dies. If they get too big or too close to Earth, they can emit enough radiation to damage our ozone layer; and moving stars, or stars that get close to our sun and interact with the Oort cloud at the edge of our solar system, which causes comets. Too many moving stars could cause a huge comet headed Earth's way.

Some of these threats are thousands of years away, but persistent research on how to survive them will be needed for future generations.[4]

as satellite images and spacecraft, to study asteroids and comets. They use these instruments and scientific data gathered from past asteroid contact to find out a doomsday rock's orbit.

When a possible doomsday rock is found, the next step is to determine when it will enter Earth's atmosphere. In July 1992, one asteroid was seen a dozen times. Scientists have a good idea of its orbit. Now they have to figure out its path around the sun. They will then know the asteroid's position for decades to come and will be able to predict whether or not it is a danger to Earth.

Is it possible to ward off a threatening space object? There are many ideas about how to save Earth from such an unwelcome visitor. Some involve the use of nuclear bombs. The people who like this idea hope that the bomb would blast the object and deflect it away from our planet. The problem is that a comet or an asteroid is millions of miles away. It is also moving extremely fast. A doomsday rock would be approaching Earth at 67,000 miles (107,803 km) per hour.

Problematic Solutions

What if we actually could bomb the threatening object? The bombs that now exist could deflect a smaller space object, but for a large asteroid, the bomb might have to be ten thousand times more powerful than any that we have at this time. How would this weapon be delivered to the asteroid or the comet? An orbiting spacecraft loaded with such a cargo could be almost as dangerous as a killer rock from space would be.

There is another problem with bombing a doomsday rock. An atomic blast might shatter it into tiny pieces, or it might break it up into several large pieces instead. These pieces could all plow into Earth's surface, causing lots of damage and killing many people.

It has been suggested that we do not actually have to bomb a doomsday rock. A nuclear bomb could be detonated miles away from the object. The radiation from the explosion would vaporize material from the surface of the asteroid, nudging it in the opposite direction. This would change the doomsday rock's velocity, altering its threatening course. Over millions of miles, that short distance would be magnified. Earth would be saved.

A comet's course could also be changed if it were hit with a huge heating device. The quickly melting ice would cause more jets of steam. Those jets might steer the comet away from Earth or slow it down. But they also might speed up the comet's journey toward our planet.

Some people are concerned that the storage and use of superbombs would be almost as dangerous as a killer rock from space. They are worried that one of them might be set off accidentally or would explode too soon. They say that the radiation from a nuclear explosion in space may put our planet in peril.

Scientists reply that there would be no more danger from superbombs than from the nuclear weapons that already exist. All such weapons are surrounded by security and have built-in safeguards to prevent any accidents. Their direction and time of detonation can be precisely controlled. A weapon directed at a doomsday rock would be detonated millions of miles from Earth. At that distance, the radiation would do us no harm.

Still, the use of nuclear weapons is enough of a worry to cause some experts to search for other methods of dealing with killer rocks from space. They suggest that a solar sail could deflect a dangerous comet. This device would catch the charged particles that stream from the sun and affect a comet's orbit. Their capture by the sail would cause the comet's path to be changed.

An orbiting mirror could focus a tight beam of sunlight on a threatening asteroid. The ray would vaporize part of the asteroid's surface. A jet of dust and ash would be created. Over months or years, that jet could shove the asteroid away from Earth. Another idea would be to use the space shuttle to place a shield in orbit around our planet.

Of course, all of these ideas have problems. Currently, one of the best methods scientists have come up with is called the gravitational tractor. This theory suggests sending a spacecraft to hover near the asteroid. The spacecraft's thrusters would angle outward from the asteroid, so they would not touch the surface.[5] The gravitational pull of the thrusters would change the asteroid's path just enough over an extended period of time to direct it away from Earth.

Another theory suggests using antimatter to deflect the killer rock.[6] All mass is composed of very small particles of matter. Each of these particles has a corresponding particle of antimatter. When matter meets antimatter, they both self-destruct in a poof of pure energy. However, no one knows how the antimatter could be delivered to the space object. Because a rocket is made of matter, it would be destroyed as soon as the antimatter cargo was loaded.

Are We in Danger?

There are plenty of ideas about how to deal with a killer rock from space. All of them would be very expensive. Even as a global society, we have limited amounts of money and resources.

During one human lifetime, there is about a one in twenty thousand chance that a mountain-sized rock will crash into Earth.

A gravitational tractor might pull an asteroid headed for Earth on a different trajectory.

During that same lifetime, a person may be killed in a car crash or be infected with a fatal disease. An 8.0 earthquake could destroy an entire city. Should we spend our money to improve driver safety, find a cure for the disease, or to find a way to predict earthquakes? Or should we spend it to outwit a killer rock from space?

Dangerous asteroids and comets are out there. Someday, one of them will be on a collision course with Earth. Perhaps for now we should just watch the skies. There are scientists around the world who study near-Earth objects (NEOs). These people are part of spaceguard associations or foundations that exist independently in many countries to help support the study of near-Earth objects. Spaceguard scientists could discover a doomsday rock early enough to prepare a defense.

In fact, on October 6, 2008, scientists using a telescope at the Catalina Sky Survey in Arizona detected the 2008 TC3 asteroid. After the small asteroid was discovered, a few other space observatories around the world followed its path and recorded data. The TC3 asteroid exploded in Earth's atmosphere the next day. Scientists were able to accurately predict the impact time and location. This was a historic moment, as it was the first time in history that an object had been observed before it was to hit Earth.

CHAPTER 5

A Cosmic Show on Jupiter

In March 1994, astronomers Carolyn (1929–) and Eugene Shoemaker (1928–1997) and David Levy (1948–) spotted a long, fuzzy-looking object in outer space. They identified the object as a comet, and it became known as Comet Shoemaker-Levy 9. The comet is as old as our solar system, and it traveled through outer space for 4.5 billion years until the sun nudged it off its usual course. Almost sixty years ago, the planet Jupiter caught the comet in its gravitational pull; every time the comet orbited Jupiter, it was drawn deeper and deeper into the planet's atmosphere. In 1992, Jupiter's gravitational force began tearing apart the icy dust ball, and its glowing string of fragments continued to orbit Jupiter.

At the time of discovery, Shoemaker-Levy 9 consisted of at least twenty-one large pieces and thousands of smaller ones. They were approaching the far side of Jupiter, the side that always faces away from Earth. All the larger pieces were on a collision course with the planet. It was predicted that the first fragment would plunge into Jupiter's gaseous surface on July 16, 1994.

This artwork shows Shoemaker-Levy 9 hitting Jupiter.

Jupiter is two and a half times larger than all the other planets combined. More than thirteen hundred Earths could be packed inside Jupiter. Astronomers believed that the large planet could easily survive the blows of the comet fragments.

They did not know what either the immediate or the long-term effects of the pummeling would be. By the spring of 1994, hundreds of telescopes on Earth were focused on the shattered comet. Cameras on board two spacecraft were set to take pictures of the collision.

Jupiter's Black Eye

On Saturday, July 16—right on schedule—the first fragment crashed onto Jupiter. The mountain-sized clump created a fireball half the size of Earth. The bubble of superheated gas was brighter than anything else on Jupiter.

The dark spots at the bottom of this ultraviolet image of Jupiter show where the fragments from Shoemaker-Levy 9 hit. These spots are dust thrown into the atmosphere by the impacts. The dark circle near the top is a shadow from one of Jupiter's moons.

By Sunday evening, seven fragments had blasted through the planet's whirling cloud cover. They were traveling at more than 130,000 miles (209,170 km) per hour, sixty times faster than the speed of a bullet. The rock-hard chunks of ice and dust had built up a tremendous energy of motion. When they hit Jupiter's wispy cloud cover, friction stopped them dead.

The smallest of the larger pieces was only a half-mile (0.8 km) wide, but it exploded with the force of 10 million megatons of TNT (one megaton is equal to a million tons). It left a spreading plume of hot gas and debris as large as Earth.

Each impact produced a mammoth fireball. The temperature at their centers was at least 53,000°F (29,000°C). The impacts left huge black scars on the far side of Jupiter. The heat was so intense that the atmosphere was speckled with many pieces of fried debris. Fiery plumes shot up hundreds of miles. The flames edged over Jupiter's horizon, where they became visible to telescopes on Earth.

On Monday morning, a 2-mile-wide (3-kilometer-wide) fragment streaked 60 miles (97 km) into Jupiter's atmosphere. Its blast was hundreds of times more powerful than the combined energy of all of our planet's nuclear weapons. The fireball it created spewed 1,300 miles (2,092 km) into space. It was fifty times more luminous than Jupiter—so bright that, for a moment, it blinded the largest telescopes on Earth.

That collision gave Jupiter a "black eye" 9,600 miles (15,446 km) across. The impact site was twice as large as Earth.

Two more fragments struck on Tuesday. The white-hot glow created by one of them was three times the size of Earth. By now, raging storms were ripping through Jupiter's atmosphere. On Wednesday, five more pieces of the dying comet added to the turbulence. They stirred up the brimstone soup of sulfur, ammonia, hydrogen, and helium. As David Levy remarked, "Jupiter has had the stuffing knocked out of it."[1]

Thursday saw the explosions of four mountain-sized fragments. They created overlapping fireballs at ten-hour intervals. The blackened impact sites were so close that they almost merged into each other.

The final large fragment struck after midnight, July 22, adding its plume to the ring of swirling, superheated gas. The comet was now completely destroyed, and, as predicted, the planet Jupiter had survived the battering.[2]

The spectacular cosmic show lasted only days, but what we learn from Shoemaker-Levy 9 will last forever.

The Future Is Unknown

What we know about threats from space is scary. Even scarier is what we still don't know; the universe is so vast that not even the most informed experts

Universal Secrets

Scientists used to believe Earth was formed by a series of gradual changes. Then they saw neatly arranged rows of craters on two of Jupiter's moons and the random scattering of craters on our own moon. With Shoemaker-Levy 9, we saw how these craters formed. It was clear the bodies in our solar system were shaped largely by stupendous explosions.

What we can learn from Shoemaker-Levy 9 goes far beyond Jupiter. Perhaps we will get a better idea of how comets formed Earth, how comets brought water to Earth, or how they brought life to Earth. The knowledge that we gain will help us better understand our entire solar system. It could give us the key to unlock some of the secrets of the universe.

know how truly large it is or what it holds. It's so big that astronomers must measure it in light-years, which, contrary to how it may sound, is a measure of distance, not time. (A light-year is the distance that a beam of light, in a straight line, travels in one year. One light-year is equivalent to approximately 5.9 trillion miles, or 9.5 trillion kilometers.[3]) Right now, astronomers can see about 13.8 billion light-years in any direction, but they know the universe is far larger than what they can see through even the most advanced telescope.[4]

Advances in science and well-trained, well-educated future generations of scientists, astronomers, and space explorers can help us learn more about the great frontier of space—and help us prepare for the threats it poses.

Chapter Notes

Introduction

1. "Severe Space Weather Events—Understanding Societal and Economic Impacts," Space Studies Board, Division on Engineering and Physical Sciences, National Research Council of the National Academies, 2008, http://lasp.colorado.edu/home/wp-content/uploads/2011/07/lowres-Severe-Space-Weather-FINAL.pdf.
2. Bonnie Sachatello-SawyerDon and Liza Charlesworth, "When Was the First Dinosaur Discovered?" Scholastic.com, https://www.scholastic.com/teachers/articles/teaching-content/when-was-first-dinosaur-discovered/ (accessed April 23, 2018).
3. "What Would Happen If an Asteroid 10 Kilometers Across Hit the Earth?" Ask an Astronomer, Cornell.edu, July 18, 2015, http://curious.astro.cornell.edu/about-us/38-our-solar-system/the-earth/impacts/51-what-would-happen-if-an-asteroid-10-kilometers-across-hit-the-earth-beginner.

Chapter 1. When Dinosaurs Roamed

1. *Britannica Library*, s.v. "Dinosaur," September 1, 2017, http://library.eb.com/levels/referencecenter/article/dinosaur/106181.
2. Lawrence Pringle, *Dinosaurs and Their World* (New York, N.Y.: Harcourt Brace, 1968), p. 38.
3. William Stout, *The Dinosaurs* (New York, N.Y.: Bantam Books, 1981), p. 4.

4. Reuel R. Hanks, “Plate Tectonics,” *World Geography: Understanding a Changing World*, ABC-CLIO, 2018, https://worldgeography.abc-clio.com/Search/Display/1665428.
5. Ian Johnston, “Asteroid That Killed the Dinosaurs Created Endless Night and 18-Month Winter as It Rained Fire,” *Independent*, August 21, 2017, http://www.independent.co.uk/news/science/asteroid-kill-dinosaurs-fifth-mass-extinction-endless-night-winter-18-month-rain-fire-ice-age-a7904491.html.
6. Ian Johnston, “Humans Are Ushering in the Sixth Mass Extinction of Life on Earth, Scientists Warn,” *Independent*, May 31, 2017, https://www.independent.co.uk/environment/mass-extinction-humans-causing-earth-deaths-end-times-warning-a7765856.html.

Chapter 2. The Tunguska Event

1. Richard Cavendish, “The Trans-Siberian Railway Completed,” *History Today* 54, no. 7 (July 2004), https://www.historytoday.com/richard-cavendish/trans-siberian-railway-completed.
2. Nigel Calder, *The Comet Is Coming* (New York, N.Y.: Penguin Books, 1980), p. 124.
3. “The Tunguska Impact—100 Years Later,” NASA, June 30, 2008, https://science.nasa.gov/science-news/science-at-nasa/2008/30jun_tunguska.
4. Britannica Library, s.v. “Space debris,” February 6, 2015, http://library.eb.com/levels/referencecenter/article/space-debris/474044.
5. Carl Zimmer, “The Smoking Crater,” *Discover,* January 1992, p. 46.

Chapter 3. Space Rocks Zooming By

1. Rogers, Paul, “Comet? Meteor? Asteroid? Here’s How to Tell the Difference,” *Mercury News*, March 10, 2013,

https://www.mercurynews.com/2013/03/10/comet-meteor-asteroid-heres-how-to-tell-the-difference/.

2. David H. Levy, *The Quest for Comets* (New York, N.Y.: Plenum Press, 1994), p. 7.

Chapter 4. Stopping a Doomsday Rock

1. David H. Levy, *The Quest for Comets* (New York, N.Y.: Plenum Press, 1994), pp. 10–11.
2. Ibid., p. 216.
3. Ibid.
4. Daniel Brown, “These Threats from Outer Space Could End Life on Earth,” *Newsweek*, January 20, 2017, http://www.newsweek.com/earth-space-cosmos-threat-end-humanity-545075.
5. Edward T. Lu and Stanley G. Love, “Gravitational Tractor for Towing Asteroids,” *Nature* 438 (November 10, 2005), http://www.nature.com/nature/journal/v438/n7065/abs/438177a.html.
6. “Vision for the 21st Century,” *Ad Astra,* June 1990, pp. 26–29.

Chapter 5. A Cosmic Show on Jupiter

1. Sharon Begley and Mary Hager, “Good Show, by Jove,” *Newsweek,* August 1, 1994, p. 60.
2. Ibid., p. 62.
3. “How Long Is a Light-Year?” NASA, accessed April 23, 2018, https://www.grc.nasa.gov/www/k-12/Numbers/Math/Mathematical_Thinking/how_long_is_a_light_year.htm.
4. Nola Taylor Redd, “How Big Is the Universe?” Space.com, June 6, 2017, https://www.space.com/24073-how-big-is-the-universe.html.

Glossary

asteroid A small planet-like object in space.

atmosphere The mass of air surrounding Earth.

BLITS Acronym for "Ball Lens in the Space," a Russian laser-ranging satellite that was thrown off course in 2013, likely because of collision with space debris.

comet A space object made of ice, gases, and dust that orbits the sun.

geology The science and study of the history of Earth and its life that is found in rocks.

gravitational pull The reaction that one object has toward another because of the force of gravity.

iridium A metal found in meteorites.

light-year A unit of measuring distance in which a beam of light, in a straight line, travels in one year.

meteor A rocky, iron, or icy object that enters Earth's atmosphere.

meteorite A stone or metallic meteor that has fallen to Earth's surface from space.

near-Earth object (NEO) An object in the solar system whose orbit brings it into proximity with Earth.

nuclear war War using weapons of mass destruction, such as atomic bombs.

Pangaea A supercontinent that existed until about two hundred million years ago, when forces such as plate tectonics caused the supercontinent to break apart, creating Earth's current continents.

radiation The process of giving off radiant energy, or heat, in the form of waves or particles.

space debris The large number of human-made objects in space, mainly around Earth's orbit; the debris ranges from tiny chips of paint to old satellites and pieces of defunct rockets.

tektite A glassy rounded object formed in the sudden heat and release of gases.

vaporize To convert to gas.

Further Reading

Books

Dickmann, Nancy. *Exploring Comets, Asteroids, and Other Objects in Space*. New York, NY: Rosen Central, 2016.

Eboch, M. M., ed. *The Next Mass Extinction.* New York, NY: Greenhaven Press, 2018.

Owen, Ruth. *Space Garbage*. New York, NY: PowerKids Press, 2015.

Pamplona, Alberto Hernández. *A Visual Guide to Space Exploration.* New York, NY: Rosen Publishing, 2018.

Websites

ESA Kids

www.esa.int/esaKIDSen/index.html

Explore the website of the European Space Agency and do activities, take quizzes, and read the latest news about Earth, the universe, technology, and life in space.

NASA Space Rocks

www.nasa.gov/audience/forstudents/5-8/features/F_Space_Rocks.html

Learn more about the different kinds of rocks from space that could hit Earth.

Index